FAIT

Faiza Ali

MAPLE
PUBLISHERS

Faith

Author: Faiza Ali

Copyright © Faiza Ali (2023)

The right of Faiza Ali to be identified as author of this work has been asserted by the author in accordance with section 77 and 78 of the Copyright, Designs and Patents Act 1988.

First Published in 2023

ISBN 978-1-83538-011-6 (Paperback)
978-1-83538-012-3 (E-book)

Photo credits on back cover:
Shiva Alaghband
www.shivaalaghband.com

Cover Design, Book Layout and Proofreading by:
White Magic Studios
www.whitemagicstudios.co.uk

Published by:
Maple Publishers
Fairbourne Drive, Atterbury,
Milton Keynes,
MK10 9RG, UK
www.maplepublishers.com

A CIP catalogue record for this title is available from the British Library.

All rights reserved. No part of this book may be reproduced or translated by any form or by any means, electronic or mechanical, including photocopying, recording or by any information storage and retrieval system without written permission from the author.

The views expressed in this work are solely those of the author and do not necessarily reflect the views of the publisher, and the publisher hereby disclaims any responsibility for them.

CONTENTS

1. Comfort 4
2. Answers 5
3. Blessed 6
4. You 7
5. Broke 8
6. Connected 9
7. You knew 11
8. Now 12
9. Race 13
10. Years 14
11. Alone 15
12. Alternative 16
13. False image 17
14. Humanity 18
15. Landed 19
16. Life 20
17. Come with me 21
18. Magic 22
19. Polished 23
20. Rain 24
21. Sometimes 25
22. Wings 26
23. Nature 27
24. Rain Drops 28
25. Zain 29

Comfort

I feel an eerie comfort in your drops,
A reminder of myself that was.
The excitement when you fall and disperse,
A fortune of freedom without laws.

The colours of the sky in your presence,
The smell of the breeze brushing past,
The elation of smiles that spread within,
The substance of life and intensity at last.

The sparkle you ignite despite the light,
I feel a storm rumbling sane.
I can inhale you with memories bright,
And for a moment forget the pain.

Answers

I simply seek answers to understand,
But why is it so difficult to explain?
Years have passed and I keep inquiring,
Until time offers a concept in vain.

I comprehend life is a critical sport,
We are only spectators in the plot.
Yet on occasion this link intimidates me,
Could this be deeper than I thought?

You conceal from yourself what I ask
Could that be why you form no reply?
Some stories are engraved into our souls,
Which we foolishly neglect and deny.

Blessed

I know you are correct,
I know you have chosen for me peace.
I know you are the divine, the almighty,
I know I should let go and release.

Why have I not learnt through the seasons,
That I have treasure in my embrace?
Why do I not value this sublimity?
Why live in memories that I retrace?

I know my character has capital worth,
I'm aware this retention is in vain,
I see decades have lapsed and I am blessed,
Why still does this distance then cause me pain?

You

Your trust elates
Your love clenching
Your gaze debates
Your smile punching

Your innocence naïve
Your intelligence sublime
Your spirit heaves
Your energy divine

Your tears lurid
Your interests thrilling
Your competitors worried
Your substance billing

Broke

So you come again to provoke me
To make me think, to invoke me?
I thought we would emerge as one,
Nevertheless you diverted and broke me.

I waited with voiceless affection to smash the shell,
To permit the breeze in where darlings dwell,
I lingered for fireflies to light the path,
Instead I glanced into the fiery glow of hell.

If I stay I promise no devotion
At the peak of it all I lost my emotion
I now seek a companion within myself
With you my spirit is of no notion.

Connected

I know not why we are connected still,
Despite setting up a pattern and accepting the stars.
Living far removed from each others existence,
Why can't these memoirs stop inducing wars?

Are your thoughts an escape from this daily course?
A fantasy to compensate from adversity I encounter?
Your regard an attempt to deny the distress of growth,
Your possibly a defence mechanism I surreptitiously mounter.

If so why daily do you entertain my thoughts?
Every song with romance whispers you near...
Closing my eyes plays trailers of your images,
My present is numb but your memory so clear...

This modern world allows you to reach me on occasion,
Why then does my heart wildly flutter?
Though the years in amidst it must beat...
Why on seeing your face do my eyes water?

I hear what you are unable to maintain,
I comprehend what you conceal through your craze.
You're trying your best to walk the right path,
Excuse my memory for interrupting your ways.

I know not why we are connected still?
A thought I can eternally ponder upon,
Our bewitching fondness confined to hollows,
Shall forever torment our hearts off and on.

… Faith

You knew

You knew what was best for me
Or so you thought.
You had a plan, to sail the sea
No idea what you sought.
I was a silly girl
Who talks to the moon,
My verdict would twirl
Not last an afternoon.
You knew you made the decision
I know how deep your regrets reside.
While catching stars was my vision
It wasn't I who needed a guide.
Love makes you powerless,
Therefore you schemed Triumph.
Do you now perceive the cowardice
Pleased with your galumph?

My shy inappropriate madness
Was where the universe hid.
Now you apprehend in sadness
But the opportunity has slid.
Your slip up was to conclude alone
How can you know what's best for me?
Those flawed in love miscarry the throne
To attain success, unity is the key!

Now

Beauty is now cosmetic,
Being prosperous judged by the bank account.
Your purity is no longer captivating,
Your character is of no surmount.

Respect is measured by education,
Popularity is based on social platforms.
Justice and human rights matter zilch,
You're not known if you fight firestorms.

Jealousy and dissatisfaction is standard,
Bribery and deceit a way of being.
Kind gestures to heal wounds is alien,
Virtues, morals and ethics are all fleeing.

Family bonds are haywire and devilish,
Washing the soul in sin is the new culture.
Why can't you love others as yourself?
Why let our ancestral efforts rupture?

You may hope but of reality be aware,
The lower world was created for a reason.
You can't be blessed with flawlessness,
People and situations change with the season.

Race

Still as a feather
Rising to fall,
Where will you go
Ends when it all?

Same illumination
Shadows are still,
I walked here once
Again I will.

Leaves, they turn
Images repeat,
Those who race
Face inevitable defeat.

Faiza Ali

Years

Years have passed and I don't understand,
Seasons turn, chapters begin and end.
You once were... Yet now your not,
So why is your essence so fresh my friend?

You chose your path, more important I guess.
I don't know if your decision has anyone to impress.
I'll have you know I'm as happy as you wished,
But my awareness is as it was, not any less.

You claimed you knew what was to come by,
You prayed diamonds and gems wipe my tears dry.
I'm waiting for the pearls of wisdom at my door,
Or atleast for my heart to comply.

Alone

Amidst this crowd bustling with support,
I realise I am alone.
They make me smile, sharing a great rapport,
Authenticity unknown.

I inaccurately believed footprints increase,
My journey is my own.
I wish I would learn to value my peace,
Have I not grown?

Within a blink loyalty perishes, friends depart,
Nothing is written on stone.
I ought to elect correct spices from the chart,
Ingredients I can loan.

Worth is all is when you discover the revelation,
Truth is shown.
The Divine gives guidance for every situation,
I am not alone.

Alternative

I never imagined an alternative
Never fathomed it barely concrete
How can an inclination so sublime
Be stranded so incomplete?

When your tower of faith collapses
Paralysis freezes each inescapable tear
Burdened in your own body
Charring your interior year by year

To place a rose on the tomb of sorrows
To rouse from the life-long trance
To glance at what has bloomed in the vicinity
To let the tears flow and advance

Opt to salute the details of what's written
Shift your anguish into ambition
Flag the power ascending in your soul
Relish in your new supreme position

I never imagined an alternative
Nonetheless I thrive in the substitute
Lilies and butterflies encircling me
This was the predestined route

False image

I hear what you say not,
Every whisper across the oceans trot.
Your words have been rather irrational,
And your behaviour absurdly international.
Be quiet and let your heart speak,
It tells me your suffering is at its peak.
You're frightened, refusing to share,
The truth may harm me so you do not dare.
Fluttering around like an injured bird,
Guilty for flying away as you preferred.
Express to me, I'll tell you it's ok,
Don't adjust to the false image you portray.
Torn between what you knew and passion,
Now you feel undeserving of compassion.
Let go my love, accept your crowd,
Believe me when I say, you make me proud.

Humanity

Where has the love gone?
What is it that you are trying to attain?
Why this petty desire to be better?
As if no humanity can now remain.

Why does the success of your brother bother you?
Why does the kindness of your sister sting?
Your miseries are not your failure
Reassess! Open your heart, let the light in.

You do not need to prove your value,
It's not necessary to visualise it a race.
End this envy competition slander and deceit,
Heal, smile, give and blossom at your pace.

Landed

I didn't realise you had landed,
You were searching for your growth's content.
You needed that stability and agreement,
I didn't realise what to you at all we meant.

Now I appreciate I was a worldly virgin,
I had not set my priorities in a mandate.
I didn't need you to boost my confidence,
I didn't need you to classify me adequate.

I sit back now and imagine you craved respect,
Yearned attention, appreciation and fame.
Selfishly you kept a hobby sidelined for an escape,
To groom yourself, recycled yet another name.

I ask, does the respect offer tranquility?
Does the silence blanket you in serenity?
Does appreciation soothe you to sleep?
Does the fame allow you to have an identity?

I hold no regret as I solemnly sought purity,
I loved not for any gain of my own.
I have now landed mixed in ways of the world,
I walk the path of petals my Divine has sown.

Life

When tears run crisp, and pain is on a high.
When Hope is lost, and trying is a lie.
You look past the mist, drenched, to dry.
You're broken but moving, logic is shy.

Paintings on a wall are yet full of content,
Nudging of a realm so energetic but still.
I wonder where to find the pieces missing.
To be in the painting, merry, at one's will.

I wished to be ignited to soar celestial,
To build memories of every jubilant fall.
But now I've forgotten what to remember,
How did my ardent world cage in so small?

Come with me

Are you not weary of living in fear?
Fear of ache and an unknown tomorrow?
Are you not fed up of fighting yourself?
Why live in entity which you borrow?

Come with me, toss your shield
Forget your worries, let candour yield
Let's walk in the meadows under the stars
Or collect fireflies in magical jars.

Social norms robbing us of choice,
Break the chains, let us rejoice.
It will work out, that's how it goes,
Without the thorns what is a rose?

Magic

Elated, upbeat or languishing,
It is I who set the ordinance!
To play the keys that be palliative,
Or to swim in a sea of despondence.

You may define sensations how you will,
My perception remains secure.
I possess power of conclusion and resolution,
I choose how I endure.

The mind conceives what you feed,
Unprofitable it is to grieve or despair.
Why not rejoice in the tear that flows?
Believe in the magic of what you bear.

Polished

For those worried about my delight,
He did not manage to take it away.
Yes, I have stumbled and crumbled,
But very in love with life I will stay.

I'm here for only but a while,
What's the aim if I squirm and scream?
Yes, I have done all of the above,
But I understand it's part of the scheme.

There is so much jubilance in this world,
A myopic vision unfocused may not see.
Every tear is a blessing in disguise,
I have been polished, this was the best for me.

Rain

Wild Rain drops blurring my windows,
Cleansing away impurities.
Creating sweet toned melodies,
Erasing lurking insecurities.

Acquainting with my solitude,
Splashing former chapters.
Charmingly asking for a dance,
Generating exquisite disasters.

The force strongly merging in,
Before the empire mislay its honour.
Impressing me to hop to the drops,
Slipping off faulty severed armour.

Sometimes

Sometimes you can't perceive what has manifested,
Sometimes it takes an era to swallow.
Sometimes your conviction can grip you so firm,
When it shatters you're unable to follow.

Sometimes you see the light and accept,
Sometimes you persevere though thoroughly shaken.
Sometimes you set new goals with blossom and colours,
Yet the spirit within you has been taken.

Sometimes you heal as your journey unbolts,
Sometimes you discover a prudent interpretation.
Sometimes you fear how you evolved,
The puzzle then no longer needs an explanation.

Wings

If I were to soar the skies an' flap my wings,
I would forget all earthly things.
Lose myself in the silver lining and beyond,
Mind empty, happy, ecstatic and not bound.

Down below there are many chains,
Gripping tight, allowing narrow lanes.
You have to abide by the laws they set,
Share your umbrella and get wet.

I have still seen flowers that grow,
Smiles that spread to and fro,
Feeding the soul confined within,
It is for that drop of hope we do not sin.

Nature

Nature has always been a healer.
For those who bled through the noise,
Isn't it the reason we inhale?
The elegance flowing eloquently with poise.

Why fight for the throne,
With drops of blood on your spoon?
Your crown is an ornament, not a rose.
A real wolf howls to the moon.

Let slip the memory of a perforated part.
Watch how the cedar tree pierces the sky.
Let go of greed and hostility,
Welcome the sun beam and identify.

Rain Drops

Rain drops, they excite,
I'm that little girl sitting by her window.
Each drop releasing a story,
Sounds promising, a melodic vow.

Time has elapsed,
Yet the little girl within me sits.
Wishing the fantasy that was to be,
Yearning for the tuneful glitz.

Reality is silence but a roar,
Innocence is beside me yet a storm.
I must hold hope to strike a chord,
Be dry in every damp form.

Zain

Your jubilance, May it last,
Your mischievous eyes and naughty frames.
Your innocence, May it be immortal,
Your talent, May it earn many names.

Your allure, May it be perpetual,
Your kindness at heart spreading grace.
Your healing touch, May it meet no end,
Your flare, May it win every race.

Your unpretentious mind, May it bloom,
Your playful channels and soft embrace.
Your entity, May it always be protected,
Your sparkle, May it conquer every race.

The book is dedicated to
Dr Mohommad Ali Khan.

Milton Keynes UK
Ingram Content Group UK Ltd.
UKHW052208031023
429856UK00020B/576